Yo

Are

Enough

By

Anthony James

You Are Enough

"A Simple Guide To Mental Well-Being"

First Edition

Copyright © 2021

Contents

Contents (continued)

Introduction

Your mental health is extremely important, without mental positivity and mental well-being life can seem like more than a struggle.

Life is often tough enough without the added strain of fighting your own demons, anxiety, stress, worry, depression and any other negative influences which your mind can manifest. This book aims to help you understand how to transform negative thoughts and emotions into positive ones, how to understand what you can control and how to address issues in your life to make positive, long lasting changes.

It is important to remember that this is a process, a journey of continual improvement and with every journey it is necessary to take the first step towards your goal. Your first step is purchasing this book, the next is reading and understanding the information, guidance and advice, followed by taking action and then repeating those positive habits until you reach your goal of mental well-being and happiness.

Your mental health is the most precious thing you have in your life and this is not a selfish statement, without your mental health and happiness how can you make others happy? How can you look after others if you are not mentally fit to do so? Ensuring that your mental health is in a positive place can actually be motivated by selfless reasons.

You already have all the tools necessary to reach mental well-being and positivity, you just need to learn how to access your greatness.

YOU ARE ENOUGH

"A problem shared is a problem halved"

Don't be afraid to speak out

It is important to learn to speak about your issues.

it's okay to not be okay.

Don't be stubborn or too proud to express how you feel, you will be surprised at how fulfilling it can be to open up and talk about what's on your mind, even if you don't receive any advice back from the person you are telling your issues to, the act of just talking about your problems can be so alleviating.

"Getting things off your chest" and talking about issues out loud can often help you process your problems and ultimately discover the potential solutions which can help resolve matters.

Don't ever think that admitting you have a problem is a sign of weakness because it takes great strength to admit that you need help.

Remember no one can promise to solve all your problems but they can promise to be there for you so you don't have to face them alone.

A problem can often get heavier if the only person carrying it is you so don't ever be too afraid or too proud to ask for help.

"One of the happiest moments in life is when you find the courage to let go of what you cannot change"

Learn to let go of things you can't control

This is probably the best piece of advice you could ever receive. Learn to let go of things you can't control, in short don't worry about the things you cannot affect.

In life you have the ability to control a number of things but there are certain elements of your life that you cannot – focus your energy and attention on the things you can control because you have the ability to change them. Focussing your attention or worrying (within reason) is actually a useful reflex, similar to fear which will make you either flee from a situation or face it head on (otherwise known as the fight or flight response), the worry reflex is useful because it drives you to change something which is of concern, however, worrying about things you cannot influence is not healthy, it is important to differentiate between the two.

Worrying about things outside of your control is extremely unhealthy often leading to sleepless nights and unnecessary stress. If something is outside of your control then learn to let it go. For example you cannot control the weather so don't worry about it, the only thing you can do is prepare for eventualities (what to do if it is sunny or raining) and so if you prepare correctly then the weather no matter what it is cannot affect your plans.

This can also apply to people's opinions of you, especially people who have never met you (they may have seen pictures or videos of you on social media and formed an opinion from this brief snapshot of your life, it is very common nowadays for people to have a preconception of you based on what they've seen on social media – which often doesn't reflect reality). Some people will hate you (it sucks but that's life unfortunately) and no matter what you do you will never change their opinion of you...... so why bother? Does their opinion help pay your bills? Does their opinion help put a roof over your head?

Learn to let that need to control things which our outside of your capacity affect your life – in most cases when you don't care about an opinion of someone and get on with your life, they actually begin to admire you from a distance.

Now it is possible to change people's opinions of you through your actions but don't make that your sole aim in life, living your life to please others (who essentially have formed an inaccurate or negative opinion of you) isn't the best use of your energy unless their opinion will help you to progress in your job or improve your life…. If their opinion of you can't help you then don't worry about it, learn to let go of these things which you can't control.

"Don't be afraid of losing people, be afraid of losing yourself by trying to please everyone around you"

Stop being a people pleaser

The great philosopher Marcus Aurelius once said "It never ceases to amaze me, we all love ourselves more than other people and yet we care more about their opinion than our own"

We discuss self-love later in this book (because not everyone loves themselves like they should), but regarding the opinion of others (mentioned in the previous section) it is important to learn not to be a people pleaser and live your life for you.

We live in a society where we are constantly influenced by judgements and opinions of others, these external opinions and judgements can trigger fears and anxiety within us. We can end up paying far too much attention to these opinions and spending far too much of our time worrying about what people think about us. For example if you lost your job you could actually spend more time worrying about what others think about you rather than actually concentrating all your efforts on finding another job and improving your circumstances. This comes from our innate desire to be loved by everyone and so we constantly seek their approval without realising how much this "people pleasing attitude" sabotages our self-confidence and contributes to our worries.

This becomes a viscous cycle because the more we seek the approval of others the more we become reliant on their approval – it's like a drug which we purchase at the expense of our own mental health.

The lesson in this section echoes the former because it's all about letting go of things you cannot control, we do not control the opinions of others, and the things we do not control are irregular. The more we keep valuing the things we cannot control then the less control we will have.
Take back control, stop pleasing others and start to please the person that matters most – **YOU**

"Increasing the strength of our minds is the only way to reduce the difficult challenges of life"

Exercise your brain

Your brain is a muscle which needs to be exercised regularly, just like any other muscle in your body – if you don't workout and exercise your body then it becomes weak, the same can be said about your brain.

Idle minds tend to develop negative thoughts and emotions – train your brain and exercise it daily. Take some time to discover what you are passionate about and channel your mind towards doing what makes you happy (things or activities which provides you with that sense of fulfilment).

Play IQ games (puzzles, crosswords, quizzes) on your mobile phone to keep your mind active and away from unnecessary negative thoughts.

Never stop exercising your brain and never stop learning - learning something new keeps life interesting, it could be something trivial or life changing but don't ever believe that you know it all and be open to learn new things. Learning keeps life exciting and discovery leads to character development, making you more interesting to others. If you close yourself off from learning then you may never find your true passion in life ...and if you are lucky enough to find your passion then be keen to learn more and achieve perfection.

"Physical strength can get you to the start line, but mental strength can get you to the finish line"

Exercise your body and meditate

Your body is almost as amazing as your mind and they often go hand in hand, a mentally healthy mind is often accompanied by a healthy body.

Physical exercise is important because it teaches us virtuous life skills such as discipline, perseverance, self-improvement, problem solving and can also help build self-confidence.

Exercising is an aspect of self-mastery.

Exercise has so many mental health benefits, it releases chemicals called endorphins that not only make you feel euphoric but reduce stress levels.

Exercise can also give you a sense of achievement, which again releases feel good chemicals in your brain and helps you appreciate yourself more for accomplishing something which makes you a better person (both physically and mentally).

Following exercise it is important to relax, warm down and destress. Do some deep breathing and meditate to empty your mind and ground yourself. Live in the present, in the moment – don't think about the past or worry about the uncertain future but be present where you are right now.

Declutter your brain and switch off from all external stimuli. Mindfulness mediation can help to slow down an overactive mind tune into your physical body.

Meditation has been proven to reduce anxiety, improve mood and improve sleep.

"There are people less qualified than you, doing the great things you want to do simply because they decided to believe in themselves"

Believe in yourself

...if you do then others will believe in you too

Self-belief is a powerful tool. We all know of people with so much self-belief that it almost comes across as pure arrogance, they are so convinced that they are the best at whatever they are doing that they succeed more than they fail, and if they fail they keep going and improving until they do succeed. They have a "never give up" attitude and all this stems from self-belief.

As previously mentioned there is a thin line between a strong sense of self-belief and arrogance but it is important to believe in yourself. Doubting yourself will most definitely result in failure, you've subconsciously preconditioned your mind that you will fail at whatever task it is that you are undertaking and convinced yourself that failure is okay because you already knew that you were going to fail. Having self-belief doesn't mean that you won't fail – it just means that you won't let failure stop you from carrying on until you succeed. Self-belief means that you back yourself to do well and you should always be the person who believes in you the most.

Self-confidence is the best outfit you can wear, so always believe in yourself. Start off with small objectives (for example it could be losing a couple of pounds of body weight and going for a 30 minute daily walk) and once you have mastered these then keep pushing yourself, using your growing self belief to achieve more.

In short **you should be your biggest fan.**

"You didn't come this far to only come this far"

Always back yourself

As mentioned in the previous section you should be your biggest fan, be your own greatest cheerleader, learn to support yourself (and your close friends) just like the celebrities you support on social media with your likes, your positive comments and sharing of their content (celebrities which you've probably never even met or had any meaningful connection with).

Put yourself in the shoes of your favourite celebrity and how you admire and support them by buying their movies, music, books or reading about their lives in a magazine. Now imagine how you would feel if you supported your own achievements and lifestyle the way you do for your favourite celebrity. You'd feel good right? So start getting into the mindset of being your favourite celebrity.

Become your best friend, encourage and support yourself to do well and succeed.

Talk to yourself like someone you love or highly respect. Learn to form a positive bond and relationship with yourself.

Give yourself words of encouragement like "You Got This!" before embarking on a challenge and back yourself to succeed.

"You have been criticizing yourself for years and it hasn't worked.

Try supporting yourself and see what happens"

Learn to enjoy your own company

If YOU don't like YOU then how can you expect anyone else to?

Learn to love your own company – spend time on your own to do the things you like to do (things which do not involve the company of others), for example reading a good book, completing puzzles (like Sudoku), fixing your car, going on a hike or playing one player video games – do whatever you are passionate about but learn to do it on your own. Learn to love being on your own and enjoying your own company, not only will this help you to not be so reliant on others (and the constant need for company) but it will also make you more attractive to be around as you will be more confident and less needy. Also self-discovery is a great thing to achieve, most people go through life not knowing who they are because they never really spend the time alone to discover themselves, they tend to go through life as a chameleon, adapting to different crowds of people to fit in and never knowing their own true identity.

❖ You have to learn to like your own company in order for others to truly enjoy being with the real you.
❖ You have to be a good friend in order to have good friends.
❖ You have to learn to love yourself in order to be loved.

Without going too deep into the topic, you have to learn to love yourself, following your own personal journey of self-discovery and self-love you should ask yourself "Would you have you as a friend?" Now the answer doesn't always have to be a resounding yes because you may have flaws which you won't tolerate in someone that you would like as a friend but being aware of these flaws is essential to self-acceptance and will lead to self-love (if you aren't there already).

Another benefit of self-love is that you will learn to care more about your own opinion than the opinion of others because you will have more respect and love of yourself over anyone else.

"You are what you believe
yourself to be"

You're in control of your inner voice

You know that voice in your head that keeps on telling you that you're a loser, that you're worthless and have nothing going for you, that voice that tells you that you can't do nothing right and you deserve to be unlucky ..... **YOU** actually control that voice....that inner voice is not a force of nature which is outside of your control and so you can change how it speaks to you.

Make that inner voice your biggest fan! Make it reinforce how good you are at things, make it constantly remind you of what successes you've achieved, make it your "hype man" for when it's time for you to shine.

It is important to work on your inner voice daily - whenever you have any negative thoughts it is important to combat them, question them and address them. Never allow negative thoughts or a negative inner voice to fester and grow stronger, remember you are the one in control.

Repeat words of encouragement and positivity with your inner voice. A good exercise to do is to set your alarm for every hour of the day and when your alarm chimes then use that moment to read an inspirational quote or to say something positive with your inner voice.

"Are the things you're doing today getting you closer to the person you want to be?"

Review your day

Reviewing your day will help you to achieve personal clarity. By assessing your daily actions and choices you will become more mindful of what can improve in your life and what to avoid in order to reduce stress and anxiety.

Taking this action a step further you can achieve a higher state of self-awareness by reviewing your daily actions and choices systematically, this activity will guide you to making better choices in the future.

❖ Ask yourself "What did you do well today?"
❖ "Which parts of your day were challenging or brought you discomfort?"
❖ "What emotions did you feel?"
❖ "What didn't you achieve today which you planned to?"
❖ "What made you feel happy?"
❖ "What can you learn from what happened today?"
❖ "What could you improve in the future?"

Daily reflection is a great method for improving mental health, it helps you to review the day and prepare for the day ahead (planning and preparation helps to reduces anxiety). Use daily reflection to assess what you did well, what makes you happy, the areas where you can improve and the planned activities that you didn't complete. This exercise will help you analyse your actions to see if they are aligned with the person you want to be or wish to become.

This daily review and analysis is essential for character development. The closer you are to being the person you want to be then the happier you will be with your life, resulting in a better mental state.

"You will never be free until you free yourself from the prison of false thoughts"

Don't overthink things

Always analyse a situation to learn from mistakes but don't dwell and rethink the scenario over and over again. You cannot change the past, once you have understood what happened and learnt from it then move on.

We've all probably experienced heart ache from a break up with someone we really liked or even loved and it is natural to rethink scenarios where you believe you could have changed the course of events and stayed together. Whilst it is important to understand where things went wrong and to also understand what you could have done differently what isn't healthy is to constantly relive or overthink these life altering scenarios. In order to heal you have to learn to move on, understand and learn but don't dwell on the past which you cannot change.

"If you want to be happy, you must be true to who you are"

Be true to yourself

Never lie to yourself, lying to yourself could lead to self-resentment, if you promise yourself you're going to do something then don't let yourself down. Always do what you say you're going to do.

This rule should not only apply to you, you should also extend this admirable trait to others. Be less of a person who talks about doing things and become a person who does the things they say they are going to do. Not only will you become someone who is reliable and respected but you will find pride in being a person who is true to their word and possessing values of this nature are extremely attractive.

Be honest! On the flipside of becoming a person who does what they say they will do, it is also important to be a person who says no to things they don't want to do... or to things they know they cannot achieve. It is imperative (as part of being true to yourself) to understand that you cannot be all things to all men but you can be upfront and honest, it is better to be realistic with people than to overpromise and under-deliver, don't say that you will do something if you can't or have no intention of doing so. Disappointing others can impact your own mental health as you will become known as someone who is unreliable and untrustworthy.

"Always plan your life around things that make you happy"

Always have something to look forward to

Whether it's a holiday abroad or simply catching up with friends at the weekend – always have something to look forward to, something that makes you get out of bed and say only X more sleeps until I'm doing X or going to X or seeing X, whatever X is – it's what helps make even the dullest day bearable. The more things you have to look forward to and the more regular these things occur then the better your life and your mental health will be.

"Make happiness a priority and be gentle with yourself in the process"

Have a routine of happiness

Prioritise being happy over everything else. If you work in a mundane and unfulfilling job then your priority should be to make money or time to do things that make you happy. Life is all about finding your happiness and once you've discovered what makes you happy then keep on doing it. So many people never invest enough time in themselves to find out what truly makes them happy - most people spend the majority of their lives working to make money thinking that this will make them happy, but it won't. Money doesn't make you happy, money is only a vehicle towards happiness. With money you are able to buy material things which may make you happy, you are able to buy experiences, create memories and also buy the time in which to find your happiness and basically live your life the way in which makes you happy.

Again, it is important to stress that working <u>to make money</u> won't make you happy, unless your work is something that you're passionate about. Being passionate about work means that it's something you'd do for free (not that you should, no one should ever work for free but the point is you enjoy it so much that it is not perceived to be what is deemed as traditional work but more like having fun and making money whilst you do it ...for example "pro video gamers", they love playing video games and get paid to do it too), however, not everyone has the luxury of working in an industry or in a job which they are truly passionate about and so it is important to focus on doing things outside of work which make you happy - use work to make money to do things which make you happy, always have these things to look forward to - whether it's living for the weekend or every evening when you get home - find that happiness within your life and access it as often as you can.

"Happiness comes from spiritual wealth not material wealth"

Money can't buy happiness

Too many people spend their lives chasing money and not living their lives or finding their happiness.

Sounds cliché but it's true, money cannot buy you happiness. What money can do is the following:-
❖ Money can buy experiences
❖ Money can buy material things
❖ Money can help you do things which create memories

But money is not the be all and end all. If you don't know what your happiness is then money is almost irrelevant. It's true, money can afford you the time to find out what makes you happy but without happiness money has next to no purpose.

"Money does not buy happiness but without money you can't buy anything.
Money buys freedom, which gives you the time to figure out what makes you happy."

I know a lot of people who aren't wealthy in terms of cash but have a wealthy mental state, they are happy and love their lives because they consistently do what makes themselves happy. On the flipside you've no doubt heard of celebrities who are extremely wealthy in terms of cash in the bank and suffering from depression, most people might question "What do they have to be depressed about?" They have money, they have fame, they can date almost anyone in the world that they like and they appear to be living a life most of us could only dream about, however, there are a number of credible reasons to why they are suffering from depression. Their depression could be because they haven't found what truly makes them happy or invested enough time in themselves to find out who they truly are – knowledge of self is important to understanding what makes you tick, what things you like and dislike, what makes you happy and what doesn't.

As previously mentioned it is also important to enjoy your own company ... a lot of celebrities spend so much time surrounded by people and also living their lives as a persona for the public that they don't know their true selves and this can often lead to depression and mental health issues.

So how can you be happy without money? It is possible but you need to find your happiness first.

❖ Time is the only thing needed to create memorable/happy experiences (money is not essential)
❖ Understanding what makes you happy is more important than having money and not knowing what to do in order to be happy

I read this quote the other day by Kevin O'Leary "A salary is the drug they give you to forget your dreams" which is kind of true but not entirely factually accurate.

Most people need a job to survive and pay bills but working a job doesn't mean that they need to forget their own dreams (just because they are getting paid to work and help to build someone else's dream).

It is also not factually accurate that working a job prevents you from building your own dream ... it just depends on how much capital/investment you need to make your dreams a reality. For example someone could have a dream to become an artist, they will initially need enough money to buy an easel, canvases, paints, brushes and potentially rent a workspace, once they have created enough artwork to showcase they will need an Instagram channel to advertise their work on and an Etsy website to sell their work from, their working capital will be relatively low in comparison to someone who has aspirations to start their own clothing company. It will be relatively easy for the artist to work a job and also build their dream in their free time.

In essence your job can be the drug which keeps you building your boss's dream or it could be the fuel you need to create your own. There was a statement which I read following the quote by Kevin O'Leary which resonated massively with me and ties in with message of this book (about improving your mental health and finding your happiness). In short it read "Doing nothing about a job you hate is unacceptable; if you hate it, change it". The same applies to your life in general – if you hate it change it.

Remember we work to live and not live to work, so live your life and start doing what makes you happy!

To summarise this section – don't feel depressed because you don't have money, work towards making money if money is what you require to find your happiness or do what makes you happy. If you have money and you're depressed then use the money to buy yourself the time needed to discover your happiness.

All you really need is time and whatever makes you happy.

"I don't care who is doing better than me, I am better than I was last year.

It's me verses me"

Stop comparing yourself to others

Comparing yourself to someone who has more than you can often lead to mental health issues, inferiority complexes and severe depression. Not everyone has the ability or the opportunities to do great things, all we can do is continue to improve ourselves both mentally and in our lives in general. It's not you verses someone else, it's YOU verses YOU.

In short, as long as you keep improving yourself then you're winning.

Don't waste energy worrying about who is doing better than you, care that you're doing better than you were last week, last month or last year.

Keep trying to be the best version of you!

Take time to reflect on where you were a year ago *"Look at how far you've come!"*

"Don't ever change to impress someone. Change because it makes you a better person and leads you to a better, brighter future"

Stop doing things you don't want to do merely to impress others

In this age of social media and the constant need for acknowledgement, followers and likes – people tend to measure their "worth" based on how many followers they have or how many "likes" their last post received. Some people may even take it as far as to quantify their self-worth based on whether they receive more "likes" or have more followers than someone else who they perceive to be their competition, as mentioned in the previous section you should never compare yourself to anyone else as we are all unique – it is "YOU verses YOU" and no one else.

It is not uncommon to see people posting on social media for "likes", for example I've seen people buying the most expensive bottles of champagne in a club just so they can post it on social media to then wake up the next day and wonder how they're going to pay for it. This behaviour is extremely unhealthy as they are not doing it to make themselves happy but to "buy" the admiration of others. It is important to understand that you can never buy affection...or if you do it can only be maintained with money, as soon as that runs out then so does the affection, attention and admiration.

Doing things solely for the purpose of attention may make you feel good in the moment but as soon as the hype dies down then most of the time you will be left thinking "was it really worth it?" Again it is important to stress that you must do things for you, things that make you develop as a person or make you happy or both. Once you began to focus on impressing yourself rather than others then not only will you be in a better place mentally but you may also impress others as a by-product anyway.
Stop doing things for "likes" unless you enjoy doing them or they pay your bills, never do anything merely to compete with or to impress someone, only do it if it makes you happy.

"When we hit our lowest point can we then open up our greatest change"

Remember the lows

This may sound strange but remembering the low points in your life will actually make the good times feel even sweeter.

You have to experience the bad times to appreciate the good times.

Nobody can go through life without having a bad day or two but remembering those lows can make the highs feel even better. The memory of a bad day or a bad experience could act as a reminder so that you avoid any actions or decisions which may result in a repeat of a negative scenario. This is how we can actually use a negative experience as a positive thing (merely because we don't ever want to be back in that dark place again). Eventually you will be able to get to such a positive mental state that you can look back at these bad times and laugh about them.

Every bad experience is one from which we can learn.

"A positive mindset brings positive things"

Fake it until you make it

The mind is a very powerful tool when used correctly. It is important to train your brain and learn how to convince yourself that you're okay with a situation until you eventually become okay with it.

Convince yourself you're fine and keep on reinforcing that point until you are. Learn how to control your thoughts and address negative thoughts (why do I feel sad? ... Identify "the why" and if you can address it then do exactly that. Example: "I feel sad because I'm worried about a bill I haven't paid", the remedy is to pay the bill as soon as you can, if you cannot afford to pay the bill then contact the debtor to make agreements to pay. Confront the problem and don't bury your head in the sand), if you cannot address the problem [Example: you are depressed because someone close to you has died, it is impossible to bring them back and so it is okay to feel sad but try not to let this consume your life] it is best to try to dismiss it from your mind until you have the tools necessary to address it, [For the example of someone close to you passing away, a tool to potentially addressing your depression could be talking about your grief with someone else or remembering the good times you had together with the person who has passed away]), it is possible with practice to completely banish negative thoughts from your brain.

Start off with small negative thoughts, a classic example is body parts. Nobody is born perfect and there are often parts of our body we would like to change, however, a better and more simple solution than going under the surgeon's knife is to become comfortable with what you deem to be a negative attribute.

Remember beauty is in the eye of the beholder and what you deem as a body defect could actually be something someone else finds appealing.

Once you've learned to love or become comfortable with what you initially perceived as being a defect then you can tackle larger negative thoughts. One of the biggest negative thoughts someone could have about themselves is believing that they are worthless, they believe they are a loser, they believe that whatever they do life will always knock them down, they believe they are destined to be unlucky throughout their lives and so they merely exist and have given up on trying to make life worth living. However, this is not the case. You attract what you project – a negative mindset will unfortunately attract negativity and a positive one will attract positivity (you've all seen or potentially know of someone who just seems to have all the good luck and on the flipside you all know or heard of someone who just cannot catch a break whatever they do they always seem to fail, this is not a coincidence, this is projection and attraction) so it is important to turn a negative mindset around.

Think like a winner and you'll soon see that your luck will turn around – believe in yourself, believe you are confident and you will succeed at whatever you do, learn to celebrate the small victories until they are merely stepping stones to the bigger victories.

Condition your brain to believe that you're okay and you are doing well through positive reinforcement, you will soon see that things will start to feel and become more positive (not only via projection but from your mental shift to seeing the positive side of things).

"Life is short, get what you can from the present but do so thoughtfully and justly"

Do what's best for you

Whichever path you are on make sure that it's the right one for you, no one can tell you what will make you happy, you need to find that out for yourself and make finding your happiness your only mission in life ….and once you've found it then do whatever it is as often as you can.

The lifestyle I'm about to describe to you may sound like a nightmare to some but a dream for others (it just depends on what you define as your ideal lifestyle, one which will make you happy) but some people are very happy with a secure job (they aren't risk takers which is fine) they love working a 9-5 and then going home to their family without having to worry about work on their own time, they are happy with their salary, the workload, the time they can take off work etc.. they are comfortable and that is enough for them to live a fulfilled life.

A person in this scenario can be in a better mental state and happier with their life than someone who runs their own business and is constantly working to make more money but then doesn't have the time to enjoy it or doesn't know what makes them happy. It just depends on what type of person you are as to which lifestyle is your dream and which is your nightmare.

I had this conversation with a man in his mid-twenties the other day. He said he wants to be rich and so I asked him why, he replied "because then I can do what I want to do" which prompted me to ask "what do you want to do?" He answered "I don't want to work for anyone and I want freedom to do what I want when I want." A good response you may think but actually he never really answered the question, he just told me what he doesn't want and that's working for someone but what does he want to do once he has money, so I asked him "what do you want to do when you're rich? What are you passionate about and what makes you happy?" He didn't know.

Sometimes it is not enough to get rid of things that don't make you happy (like working a job) because a job keeps your mind occupied for 8 hours of the day, whereas imagine having 8 hours more a day of free time and not knowing what you want to do with it? Sure, money can help you buy experiences, you can travel the world and never have to worry about paying bills again for the rest of your life with financial freedom but then what? What are you actually going to do with your life? You could maybe work for yourself but again what are you passionate about? I've started a number of businesses because I've identified gaps in the market and believed making money and being my own boss would make me happy but it didn't because I wasn't passionate about the jobs or the industry even though there were opportunities to make money. After a while I got the Monday morning blues (and I was my own boss), I began to hate my own business and was merely going through the motions until I couldn't take it anymore and sold up. So even being your own boss and making money doesn't guarantee happiness.

Finding your happiness must be your priority. Do what's best for you!

"Being happy is a personal thing and it has nothing to do with anyone else"

Don't follow the rules unless they make you happy

Society will dictate what you should do and when you should do it. For example in the western world, society dictates that you should be married in your twenties or early thirties and also have kids in your thirties at the latest. Society also dictates that you should stop going to nightclubs in your early thirties or else you will look out of place etc... but why? Who has decided that these unwritten rules should apply to all? If you want to still go to nightclubs in your fifties because you enough the music, the atmosphere, dancing and drinking then do it! Forget what anyone else thinks.

If you want to start a family later on in life because you want to make money and plan or you haven't found the right person to settle down with then do it.

No one should dictate when you should do anything and no one should define your happiness. As long as it doesn't break the law then do whatever puts a smile on your face even if it doesn't conform to what is deemed as the norm.

Why conform to the norm, when normal is "safe", "mundane" and "boring" – you are unique and so life your own unique lifestyle.

Someone asked me "What am I going to do when I get to the top?"
I replied, "Reach down and help others up"

Find happiness in making others happy

It's amazing what a smile can do, the simple action of smiling is extremely powerful and can instantly make you feel better, try it!

Just smile now for no reason and see how you feel, amazing right?

Now extend that joy to others (I don't mean in a creepy way where you walk around with an inane grin on your face for the rest of the day but) when the moment arises give someone who may be a complete stranger a smile.

For example if you are passing someone in the street and you happen to catch their eye instead of staring back completely expressionless try a simple smile where appropriate, you will be surprised at the effect that can have both on the person you share the smile with as well as yourself for making someone's day, it can be extremely rewarding.

A smile is extremely powerful so use it.

Once you've worked on your own happiness and mental health it is important to find happiness in helping others and spreading the joy you've managed to discover.

There's nothing more rewarding than helping others once you're in a position to do so.

"To find peace you have to be willing to lose your communication with people, places and all things that create the noise in your life"

Find your peace

"A break from someone or something will either make you realize how much you miss them or how much peace you have without them".

The older you get the more you will realise that you don't want conflict, drama or stress. You just want to be at peace with yourself and others, comfortable, stress free and constantly happy.

Finding your peace may coincide with being at ease or comfortable with your own company and self-love but you can also "find your peace" when in the company of others (it just means being away from all elements of drama and stress). It is the moment when you are content with everything and you are mentally in a good place.

Meditation is a good way to find your peace, clear your mind of all stress and worry to just be in the moment, however this method does not work for all and you have to find out what works best for you - it might be as simple as taking a bath with some candles and lavender or having a quiet drink with close friends reminiscing about old times, whatever activity it is which makes you feel whole and content is what you need to identify.

"Today's a new day, a new hope, a new blessing, it's your day, you shape it. It's a new chapter in the book of your life, so make it a good one"

A new day is a new beginning

"This is the first day of the rest of your life!"

Always wake up with a positive attitude and use every morning as a fresh start, use your sleep as a way to reset any negativity from the day before. If you start your day with a positive mindset you will be surprised at how much better your day will be than if you started it off in a bad mood.

Also get into the everyday habit of making your bed in the morning, get into the habit of good routines.

Making your bed everyday is something which is rewarding and starts you off in a positive mindset, even though it is a small act, making your bed is an early daily statement of "doing things and accomplishing objectives".

At the very least if you have a bad day then you'll have a nicely made bed to climb into at the end of it (so that you can wake up refreshed and ready to go again tomorrow).

"*Your vibe attracts your tribe*"

Surround yourself with people who are positive but also people who you wish to emulate

If you surround yourself with bums the most likely outcome is that you will be a bum too. It's only in very rare cases that someone who grows up in such an environment makes it good, hence the reason why there are so many "Rags to Riches" stories (or stories where someone defies all the odds to overcome their environment to succeed) which do well at the movies.

If you wish to achieve happiness and mental wellbeing then surround yourself with people who provide you with those positive vibes, do not be afraid to cut people off who affect your mental health in a negative manner … they will find their tribe, you must be selfish and find your own. If you feel depressed after a conversation with someone then it is most likely that you aren't compatible and you should cut them out of your life; it is important to be with and interact with people that light up your soul, that make you feel alive, happy, revitalised, people that bring out the best in you, people that you miss when they are not around, people that drive you to be the best version of yourself, people that positively impact your life.

Don't get me wrong, there are some people out there who get a sense of fulfilment picking people who are depressed up, those people tend to be mentally strong and their happiness comes from helping others, if you are one of these people then you are part of a tribe where you are the rock and help others to become the best version of themselves …but if that's not you then do what's best for you. Everybody has a role and a purpose in this world — so don't feel guilty about cutting people who aren't good for your mental health or your soul out of your life, they will find their tribe.

Successful people surround themselves with other successful people – it is true "success breeds success" for example, if you want to be successful investing in stocks and shares then surround yourself with people who have been there and done that, people who are still reaping rewards and making savvy investments, people which you wish to learn from.

These same rules also apply to your mental health.

"Every one of us is an inspiration to someone. A role model can show you what's possible through actions, values and behaviours"

Find inspiration in others

This is not a contradiction of the section which advised you not to compare yourself to others, by finding inspiration from others you are not comparing yourself to them but merely using them and their experiences as an example.

Some people may have been through similar situations and hardships to yours and come out the other side successfully, for example look at Tyson Fury – he suffered from mental health issues, depression, drug and alcohol abuse, he become overweight and suicidal but then turned his life around and became heavyweight champion of the world.

Often we focus so much on our own problems that we don't notice that there are others suffering the same hardship and people who have been through the hardship (we are experiencing) and come out the other side.

Social media can often be a toxic environment but there's also some good which can come from it. It is a place where you can find people who have experience of dealing with the issues you currently have and they can guide you through the hardship.

If you can't find someone who can help you through a situation then you can gain inspiration from similar stories which people share about their past, stories which may comprise of more tragic circumstances than your own.

If they can get through it then so can you, let them inspire you to get better and be better.

"If you want something you've never had, you have to do something you've never done"

Read inspirational quotes

Read inspirational quotes daily or whenever you need a reminder to stay focus and keep going "You've got this!"

Quotes like:-

"Be proud of yourself for all those silent battles that you've fought, all those times when you 've been knocked down and decided to get back up. You're a warrior!"

There are a number of inspirational quotes to be found online.

"Remember to celebrate the milestones on the road ahead"

Celebrate your achievements

You have to celebrate achievements whenever you can, enjoy these milestones and use that success to drive you on to achieve more, remember the feeling of winning or celebrating an achievement and use that as fuel to keep going.

Now it is important to not celebrate everything, just celebrate results! For example don't celebrate signing up for the gym in January and then never actually going but celebrate going to the gym and doing your first session and then losing that stone which was your first target. Celebrate milestones and results and not the planning or thought of taking action.

"You either succeed or you learn, you only fail when you quit"

Try not to have regrets

We all make mistakes but you must learn not to dwell and lament over these bad decisions but process and learn from them.

I remember when I was younger, I was a student at university and had a crush on one of the girls on my course. One night (towards the end of our degree) we were all on the town together for a night out, however I didn't notice the subtle signs of my crush flirting with me. It was only once we'd graduated and moved on that one sleepless night (while my mind was overthinking things) the realisation hit me but it was too late, she was happily involved with someone else and I was left wondering "What if".

"What If" is the worst questions to ask following a bad decision or life choice. It is hard not to think retrospectively in these circumstances but it is important to not ask "What if" as you cannot change the past, a better and much more constructive question to ask is "What can I learn from this experience", don't regret that it happened because you can learn from it.

So try not to have any regrets, only lessons which you can learn from. You have to condition your mind to not be idle, because idle minds will overthink things, wander to negative places or dwell on bad decisions without trying to learn from them.

Don't allow time for regret, we move on because we are accepting of what we are and not what we think we should be, it's hard (and will take a lot of effort and mental strength) but you have to forgive yourself and move on. Try not to think "what if" because that time has past, it is better to understand what you can learn from the experience and then you will have the knowledge necessary to cope with a similar situation should it arise in the future.

"Solve the problem or leave the problem but don't ever live with the problem"

Learn to problem solve

When we are faced with a problem our natural response is to panic, however it is important to learn how to take a step back from the situation and think of logical steps to take in order to solve the problem. Panic cannot help you resolve the problem, it is merely the emotion which drives you to find a solution.

As previously mentioned in this book, not every problem can be solved by you (which is fine), you have to differentiate between the things you can change/control and the things which you cannot. Once you have an understanding of what you can control then you can plan a path to resolving those problems.

I like to think of every eventuality for a problem and so I am prepared for whatever outcome may occur.

For example, I once had a business and a business partner who decided one day that we couldn't continue working together and said that we should part ways but he wanted to keep the business and for me to depart but I didn't want to do that. So in my mind there were only 3 possible ways forward:-

1. He leaves the business
2. I leave the business
3. We agree to put aside our differences and continue to work together

Once I had made peace with every possible outcome then I was happy to lay all my cards on the table and let him decide on how we should proceed. This skill of problem solving and anticipating every eventuality is extremely important because it reduces anxiety and helps mental well-being (as there are little or no surprises once you've thought of every potential outcome to a problem).
Once I had undergone this process, the sleepless nights stopped and so did my anxiety regarding the issue.

"Everything in life is temporary, especially the bad times so keep going"

Everything is momentary

Worry is what occurs when your mind dwells on negative thoughts, uncertain outcomes or thinks about things that could potentially go wrong. Worrying stimulates your brain to try to keep you safe, it is completely natural to worry.

Excessive or persistent worrying is where this emotion can become unhealthy. Constantly thinking about "what ifs" and "worst case scenarios" will take a toll on your emotional and physical health. It is important to understand that everything is momentary, what seems like a huge problem today will be old and familiar in the future.

Think about where you are now and what you've had to overcome to get here, think of how much you worried over an exam you took when you were younger and how that emotion is now a distance memory.

So instead of excessive worrying it is important to try to keep calm and think beyond the problem or issue as everything is momentary. The moment or situation that you are worrying about will pass, try to think beyond that moment and visualise yourself on the other side. You've been in situations like this before and come out the other side, use the memory of these moments to get past your current adversities.

We've all experienced extremely difficult situations, dark moments in our lives which we can look back on and potentially joke about, especially now that they are behind us.

Just remember every dark moment is just another one of these incidences which will pass. Nothing is permanent, everything is momentary.

"Nobody watches you harder
than the people that don't like you
or want to see you fail.
So give them a show"

Use hate as fuel

This section can be viewed as quite controversial but if you can use negative energy to achieve positive things then I believe it is a good feature to add to your mental health arsenal.

If people dislike you for achieving your dreams or working towards your dreams then use that hate as fuel to achieve more and do better. Make it a mission to post your success for them, be successful for the people who wanted to see you fail.

Sometimes it can be a sad world which we live in, where people want to see others fail – unfortunately this negativity cannot be avoided but you don't have to let it get you down or get in the way of your mental health, your successes and your potential greatness.

Use these negative feelings and comments aim at you as fuel, if someone says "you'll never find happiness" then make it your goal to prove them wrong and in so doing you WILL find your happiness.

.

"The real value of setting goals is not the recognition or reward, it's the person we become by finding the discipline, courage and commitment to achieve them"

Set goals

...but make the steps towards these goals small and achievable.

If a goal seems too daunting then you may not even begin to tackle it, you have to make the steps small and achievable so that you can see a clear and easy path towards your end goal. For example if you plan to make a million dollars in the next year that could seem like a daunting task depended on your financial situation, however, if you devise a plan of action with achievable milestones (plot the steps you need to take from your current position until your goal and keep simplifying the actions you need to take) you will make the overall objective much less daunting.

The number of steps in your plan will grow as you simplify the actions you need to take, it is important to keep expanding the plan until you have a clear roadmap from where you are now to where you want to be.

You will be surprised at how simple the first action could be to achieve your end goal, the first step could be something as simple as writing an email.

Goals are important because they give us something to focus on, something to look forward to and a sense of purpose to our lives.

Aim for the stars and even if you only reach the moon, you still have achieved something great.

"Happiness always comes from within. It is found in the present moment by making peace with the past and looking forward to the future"

Conclusion

Hopefully this book has given you an outline and some guidance into finding your peace, your happiness, provided you with methods to protect your mental health and develop mental strength.

Hopefully it has helped you to understand what you can control and what is just noise. It has helped you to find self-love and plot a path to an improve life.

Following the analysis of the content of this book, nowhere should feel more peaceful, more free of interruptions, than your own soul. Retreat to consult your own soul and then return to face what awaits you – with belief, vision and mental strength to overcome all adversity.

We all need to take the steps necessary to improve ourselves every day in terms of our mental health, mental strength, knowledge and general lifestyle. We should use the lessons in this book to work on our mental wellbeing until we are able to look ourselves in the mirror and ask "Are we happy, truly happy?" and reply with our inner voice

"YES I AM! BECAUSE I AM ENOUGH".

.

Printed by Amazon Italia Logistica S.r.l.
Torrazza Piemonte (TO), Italy

28514013R00050